Peter & the Wolf

Serge Prokofiev's story illustrated with designs by Professor Nicola Benois

for the ballet production at

La Scala

with special thanks to Nikita Lobanov

text by David Brownell, drawings by Nancy Conkle

Here is Grandfather's house

where Peter lived.

Peter

Early one morning Peter opened
the gate and went out into the big
green meadow.

The Bird - a Flute

(But this really seems to be a recorder.)

On the branch of a large tree sat a little bird, Peter's friend. "Everything is quiet," chirped the bird gaily.

The Duck - the Oboe

Soon a duck appeared, waddling from side to side. It was glad that Peter had not closed the gate, and it decided to take a nice swim in the deep pond in the meadow.

The Bird - more Flutes

Seeing the duck, the little bird flew down upon the grass, settled next to the duck, and shrugged its shoulders.

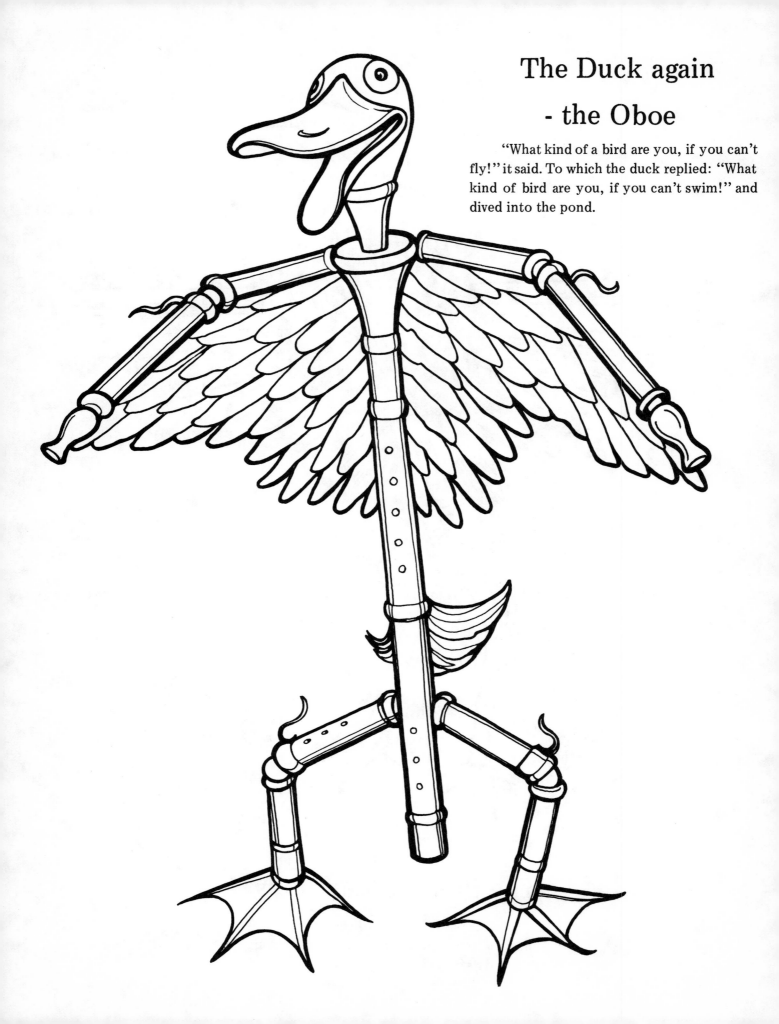

The Duck again
- the Oboe

"What kind of a bird are you, if you can't fly!" it said. To which the duck replied: "What kind of bird are you, if you can't swim!" and dived into the pond.

The Duck and a Duckling

They argued and argued—the duck swimming in the pond,
the little bird hopping along the bank.

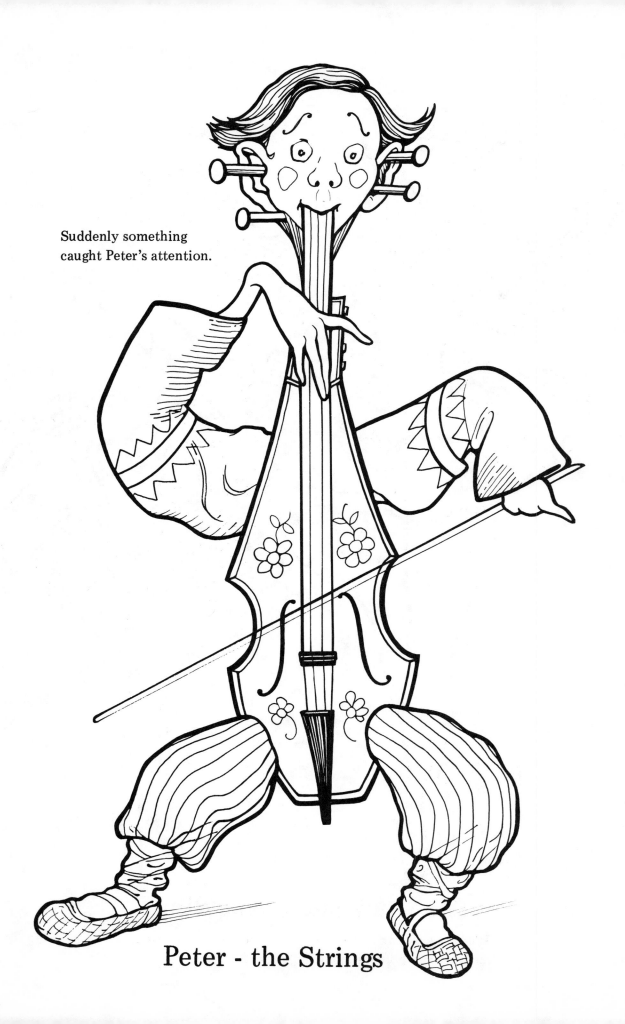

Suddenly something
caught Peter's attention.

Peter - the Strings

The Cat - a Clarinet

He noticed a cat slinking through the grass.

The cat thought, "The bird
is busy arguing. I'll just grab it."
Stealthily it crept toward the
bird on velvet paws.

The Cat

"Look out!" shouted Peter, and the bird immediately flew up into the tree, while the duck quacked angrily at the cat ...from the middle of the pond.

Peter

The cat walked around the tree and thought, "Is it worth climbing up so high? By the time I get there the bird will surely have flown away."

Grandfather came out. He was angry because Peter had gone past the gate into the meadow. "It is a dangerous place. If a wolf should come out of the forest, what then?"

Grandfather

Peter paid no attention to Grandfather's words:

boys like him are not afraid of wolves.

Grandfather again
- a Bassoon

But Grandfather took Peter by the hand, led him home and locked the gate fast.

The Wolf

And indeed, no sooner had Peter gone, than an enormous grey wolf came out of the forest.

The duck quacked and in its excitement jumped out of the pond, to run away.

The Wolf again

- 3 French Horns

The cat quickly climbed up the tree.

But no matter how hard the duck tried, the wolf ran faster. He was getting nearer. . . nearer. . . catching up with the duck. . . and then he caught it. . . and with one gulp, swallowed it.

And now, this is how things stood: the cat was sitting on one branch . . . the little bird on another . . . not too close to the cat.

And the wolf prowled round and round the tree looking at them with greedy eyes.

The Wolf - 3 French Horns

In the meantime, Peter, without the slightest fear, stood behind the locked gate watching all that was going on.

He ran home, got a strong rope and climbed up the high stone wall.

One of the branches of the tree around which the wolf was walking stretched out over the wall.

Grabbing hold of the branch, Peter climbed over onto the tree.

Peter said to the little bird: "Fly down and circle around the wolf's head, only take care that it doesn't catch you."

The little bird almost touched the wolf's head with its wings while the wolf snapped angrily at it from this side and that.

How the little bird did worry the wolf! How the wolf wanted to catch it! But the little bird was clever, and the wolf simply couldn't do anything about it.

Note: this one crucial scene is not by Prof. Benois, but shows how it was illustrated in Moscow.

Meanwhile, Peter made a lasso with the rope and, carefully letting i

...own, slipped it over the wolf's tail and pulled with all his might.

Feeling itself caught, the wolf began to jump wildly trying to get loose. But Peter tied the other end of the rope to the tree.

A Hunter - a Kettledrum

The wolf's jumping only made the rope around its tail tighter.
Just then, out of the woods came the hunters.
They were following the wolf's trail and shooting as they went.

A Hunter

A Hunter

the Bass Drum

But Peter, sitting in the tree, said: "Don't shoot! The little bird and I have already caught the wolf. Help us take it to the zoo."

The Hunters - the Bass Drum

Imagine the triumphal procession: Peter at the head.
After him, the hunters were leading the wolf.

Another Hunter   a Kettledrum

Grandfather   a Bassoon

And, winding up the procession, Grandfather and the cat. Grandfather tossed his head discontentedly: "Well, and if Peter hadn't caught the wolf? What then?"

The Bird

Above them all the little bird, chirping merrily: "My, what fine fellows we are, Peter and I! Look what we have caught!"

And, if you listen very carefully, you could hear the duck quacking inside the wolf's stomach, because the wolf had been in such a hurry that it had swallowed the duck alive.

The Bird

Above them all the little bird, chirping merrily: "My, what fine fellows we are, Peter and I! Look what we have caught!"

And, if you listen very carefully, you could hear the duck quacking inside the wolf's stomach, because the wolf had been in such a hurry that it had swallowed the duck alive.

A Lesson

The Story of the Story

One winter day in 1935, in Moscow composer Sergei Prokofiev took his wife Lina and their two sons, Svyatoslav, 11, and Oleg, 7, to see an opera for children, *Fisherman and Goldfish*, put on by the new Moscow Theatre for Children. After the show, the Prokofievs talked with Natalie Staz, a thirty-year-old actress who helped run the company. She was grateful that Prokofiev was too polite to tell her what she knew—that the show wasn't very good.

A week later the Prokofievs returned to see the next production. This time Natalie Staz sat with them in their box. She reported that Prokofiev's "unusual appearance in a foreign-made suit of a sandy-red color, his sparse reddish-blond hair, rosy cheeks, rimless eyeglasses, and rare smile led one of the young actresses to remark, 'He looks like the fourth from his *Three Oranges*'" (referring to Prokofiev's opera, *The Love for Three Oranges*). Prokofiev told Staz that he liked the idea of musical theatre for children, but he didn't feel that her shows were the sort of thing the children really liked.

Later, in March 1936, Prokofiev came to another production. He was alone, his wife and sons having returned to Paris, the family's home. He noticed that what seemed to interest the children in the audience most was the opportunity to look at the instruments in the orchestra. When Prokofiev congratulated the performers backstage after the show and commented on this, Natalie Staz decided that this was the moment to ask him to compose a work for the group. She suggested a symphonic fairy tale, to introduce children to the musical instruments.

Prokofiev asked for time to think about the idea, then met again with Staz. "We would have to find some 'images' that will be easily associated with the characteristic sounds of the instruments," he said.

"How about. . . the flute as a little bird?" Staz suggested, rather afraid that the great composer would think her idea too simple-minded.

"Absolutely. We should not be afraid of the most elementary childish fantasy. The most important thing is to find with them a common language."

"Perhaps it would be good," suggested Staz, "to have a number of animals and birds in the composition, and at least one person."

Prokofiev nodded. "But if we designate one instrument to the role of each animal, then the 'image' of a person should be performed by, let's say, a string quartet. Of course, we have to start with something concrete, something with contrasts easily understood by a child: a wolf—a bird, good—evil, something big—something small. And each one should have its *leitmotif* " (a recognizable tune associated with a character or idea in the story).

Prokofiev agreed to write a piece; the theatre would pay him whatever it could scrape up. Staz asked a poet friend to write a story for the symphonic fairy tale, but Prokofiev found this story useless. He decided to make up his own, which he called "Petya (little Peter) Fooled the Wolf." He wrote, "What was important to me was not to tell a story but to have the children listen to the music, for which the story was merely a pretext."

Like many composers, Prokofiev worked at the piano, figuring out his basic melodies and writing them down in the form of a piano score. The last part of his job would be orchestrating the score—assigning different tunes to the different instruments. But he must have made most of these decisions already in his mind.

When he finished the piano score, Prokofiev and Staz took a group of children away from rehearsing another work, and Prokofiev played the piano version for them while telling them the story, to see how they would like it. The children wanted the story to be more exact—"What kind of bird is it?"

Serge Prokofiev & the Children

A week later Prokofiev finished orchestrating his score. The first performance was May 5, 1936: the children in the audience were shown the instruments of the orchestra first, and introduced to their sounds. Then the piece was played, and everyone loved it.

After this success, it was repeated often. In July 1936 Lina Prokofiev, Svyatoslav, and Oleg were in the audience, having come to live in Moscow permanently. "*Peter and the Wolf*," said Prokofiev, "is a present not only to the children of Moscow, but also to my own."

One thing had marred the opening for Prokofiev: Natalie Staz was not the narrator. Prokofiev was told she was "unavailable." Several months later she was swallowed up by the great Russian wolf—arrested and sent to a labor camp in Siberia. Why?

At this time Soviet ruler Joseph Stalin was directing a great purge of Russian society. Prominent people in every field, and unknown ones as well, were arrested. Many were forced to confess in public trials; others simply disappeared. Staz had been the wife of Marshal Mikhail Tukhachevsky. As part of Stalin's attack on his own army, he arrested Tukhachevsky, tried him, had him convicted of treason, and executed him. Staz, his wife, was guilty by association.

Composers and theatre people were also affected by the purge trials, since in Soviet Russia all forms of artistic activity were considered the state's business. At the time Prokofiev decided to write *Peter and the Wolf*, the state's attention had turned to composers. In January 1936, the attack had begun on composers accused of the crime of "Formalism"—the most prominent being young Dmitri Shostakovich, whose works Prokofiev had praised.

Dmitri Shostakovich

No one knew quite what "Formalism" was, and this made composers all the more fearful of being accused of it: how could you prove you weren't guilty of "Formalism" if no one knew what it was?

The president of the composers' union tried to define the crime: "Every composition should be considered Formalistic in which the composer fundamentally does not have as his aim the presenting of new social meaning, but focusses his interest only on inventing new combinations of sounds that have not been used before. Formalism is the sacrifice of the ideological and emotional content of a musical composition to a search for new tricks in the realm of musical elements—rhythm, timbre, harmonic combinations, etc."

Serge
Prokofiev

Prokofiev defended Shostakovich against this state-inspired attack, saying, "In our country everything that is not understood at the first hearing is condemned as 'Formalistic.'" In response, the critics turned on Prokofiev, and much of his early music was pronounced "Formalistic" and banned from being played.

It seemed that to be safe a composer had to demonstrate that his heart was in the right place, and to try to sound like everyone else. Perhaps one reason Prokofiev chose to write for children was a desire to find a subject no one could object to.

Prokofiev's next subject also seemed safe: to celebrate the twentieth anniversary of the Bolshevik Revolution, he put music to text by Marx, Lenin, and Stalin, and included sounds of artillery, machine guns, and sirens. The subject matter didn't save the music from being pronounced "Formalist."

Prokofiev next made an opera from a novel with the safe title, *I Am a Son of the Working People*. The opera, *Semyon Kotko*, was to be directed by Prokofiev's old friend Vsyevolod Meyerhold, whose theatre had been shut down during the purge trials. But in June 1939 Meyerhold, then 68, spoke before the First National Convention of Theatrical Directors, asserting that every director must have the right to experiment, "the moral right to test his creative ideas, the right to make mistakes."

What, he asked, was this "Formalism?" He told his hearers to go look at "the colorless, boring productions which were all alike and had lost their own individual creative signature."

"In the very places where only recently a creative life was seething, where men of art were searching, making mistakes, experimenting, and finding new ways to create productions, of which some were bad and others magnificent, now there is nothing but a depressing, well-meaning, shockingly mediocre and devastating lack of talent. Was this your aim? If so, you have committed a horrible crime. In your effort to eradicate 'Formalism,' you have destroyed art."

After this, of course, Meyerhold was not "available" to direct Prokofiev's opera. It was staged badly by a mediocre director with no offensive ideas. Meyerhold was arrested for counter-revolutionary activities. His wife was knifed to death in their apartment; Meyerhold was shot in a labor camp in 1942.

Prokofiev himself was denounced several times; many of his works were banned from performance. Under the circumstances, he could not write more works for children. The state divorced him from his wife when it made illegal all marriages between Soviet citizens and people of foreign birth (she had been born in Spain). Lina Prokofieva was sent to a labor camp. Prokofiev survived, but lived under the threat of state interference and disapproval until the day of his death—the day Stalin died, also.

Prokofiev's music has survived, however. The composer, like Peter, may not have known there were dangerous wolves in the world, but sometimes innocents outlast wolves.

About the Instruments

Prokofiev meant *Peter and the Wolf* for an audience who could see the musicians playing. But if you listen to a record and use your ears carefully, or, better yet, follow a score as well, you can learn a great deal about the sounds of the instruments even without seeing the orchestra. Nicola Benois' witty drawings also show you something about the characters and the instruments that portray them.

Prokofiev used the usual string section—first and second violins, violas, violoncellos, and double basses. The wind instruments are a flute, an oboe, a clarinet, and a bassoon. The horns are a trumpet, three French horns, and a trombone. Two percussionists play all the instruments Prokofiev calls for; one plays the kettle drums, triangle, tambourine, and cymbals; the second, the castanets, snare drum, and bass drum. Prokofiev was writing for a small theatre orchestra, and also, by using a small orchestra, allowing his child listeners to hear the individual instruments.

Particular instruments play the leitmotifs associated with each character. Peter, for instance, has a theme played by the string section. Accordingly Benois shows him playing a violin, then with the body of a cello.

The string instruments of the orchestra have existed more or less the way they now are since the Middle Ages. By 1600 the great age of instrument-making began. Until about 1750 in Cremona, Italy, the Amati family, of whom Niccola was the last and best, Niccola's pupil, Antonio Stradivari (1644-1737), and Giuseppe Guarneri (1687-1742) made instruments which are still played, and are still regarded as the finest in the world. The bows used, however, are a little more recent: the modern bow was developed by Francois Tourte, who lived from 1747 to 1835.

Violins have four strings, tuned in fifths, and usually made of wire or gut. To tune them, you tighten or loosen them by turning the pegs on the neck. A violinist may have to replace a string as often as once a week, as rarely as once a year. Have you ever seen what happens when a violinist performing a solo with an orchestra breaks a string during a performance? He borrows the violin of the concert-master, the leader of the first violins; the concert-master borrows the violin of the performer behind him, and each in turn borrows from his junior behind him until the lowest-ranking man at the back is left with nothing to play.

The Violin

The noise a violin makes is produced by setting the strings vibrating by scraping them with the horsehair on the bow. The violinist shortens the strings by holding them against the fingerboard on the neck of the violin with the fingers of his left hand to make the strings the proper length to produce the notes he wants. Strings are tuned E, A, D, G. The body of the violin exists to amplify the sound made by the strings, which make the rest of the violin vibrate.

Second violins have the same body and tuning as the firsts.

The viola, the next of the string instruments, is held under the chin like the violin. To have the best possible tone for its tuning, it would need a larger body—an awkward size, between the violin and the cello, too big to tuck under the chin, not quite large enough to stand on the floor. To avoid this awkwardness, the viola remains its present size, which gives it a veiled, throaty sound. Violas are tuned one-fifth below the violin—as if you took away the top string from the violin, and put on a new bottom one. A violist needs large, flexible hands, as the left hand makes large stretches on the viola, and the strings, thicker than those of the violin, require more pressure.

Deeper still in sound is the cello, or violoncello, to be formal about it. Its four strings have a range of three and a half octaves. The thick strings and large fingerboard call for a wide variety of pressures and positions, and very agile bowing. As late as the eighteenth century, the instrument was not standardized: Bach wrote cello sonatas for his own five-string instrument. A cellist sits with the instrument between his legs, and fiddles across it. The idea seems obvious, but for years no one thought of adding the tail-pin, which reaches from the cello bottom a foot down to the floor, to rest the weight.

The remaining string instrument is the one that is left out of string quartets, but sometimes shows up in country music groups or jazz bands. The bass, or double bass, or contrabass, or bass viol, or bull fiddle, joined the family late. In the sixteenth century, most composers only used it for novelty noises—storms and tempests. Not until 1757 did one join the orchestra of the Paris Opera. The strings are five to six times as long and thick as those of the violin, and playing the bass takes heavy pressure on the four strings (E, A, D, and G). Only pegs with worm gears can exert pressure enough to stretch the thick strings into tune. Bass players have hard luck hitch-hiking.

Peter's friend the bird is represented by a flute. If you want to see how a flute makes sounds, try blowing into a coke bottle. Your breath sets a column of air vibrating. The flute, like other wind instruments, is just a container for a column of vibrating air, made in a way such that the player can vary the length of the column. The larger and longer the column, the deeper the tone.

Flutes have existed for many years, but have changed a great deal during that period. In the late seventeenth century a flute had three pieces, with six fingerholes and one key, which opened a hole usually closed. (Whenever a player closes a hole, he lengthens the column of vibrating air.)

The Flute

The Ce

The man who made the first modern flute was Theobald Boehm (1794-1881) of Munich. Boehm changed the bore of the flute from a conical one to a cylindrical one; then he enlarged the holes, and moved them to the proper places to produce pure, accurate sound. Of course, now the holes were too big to be covered by fingers, and were placed so that no hand could reach them all at once. So Boehm invented a new system with keys by which the flutist's fingers could work rings and covers over the holes. Older flute players didn't like Boehm's flute: to use it, they had to relearn their fingering from the beginning. But its advantages were so great that it became the standard.

Just to complicate things, Benois' bird isn't playing a flute at all, but some sort of recorder. The flutist puts his mouth at the side of one end of the flute, and holds the body out to the side of his face. The fit of his mouth on the mouthpiece is important: that, and the way he uses his tongue (double- and triple-tonguing, it's called) enable him to achieve some sounds. All this is called embouchure: if you can catch a flutist with his flute, get him to show you what he does.

The duck is represented by the oboe, one of the wind instruments with a reed in it. The oboe, English horn, bassoon, and contra-bassoon are double-reed instruments; the clarinet and saxophone use a single reed. A double reed is a thin piece of wood, rather like a doctor's tongue-depressor, split in half so that the two halves can vibrate against each other. As the performer's breath passes over the double reed, it vibrates the reed, producing the sound, which the instrument refines. Performers whose instruments use reeds spend much of their time fiddling with their reeds—pruning them to size and shape, keeping them moist, changing them, and just worrying about them. Often you'll see they have a small glass of water beside them—it's for the reed, not the reed player.

In Shakespeare's time the oboe was spelled "Hautboy," but pronounced as it is now. Renaissance and eighteenth-century composers used oboes, but the present form of the instrument dates from the nineteenth century, with many improvements made between 1825 and 1882. Boehm's ideas for the flute were adapted to the oboe: by 1825 it had ten keys, by 1840, fourteen. The 1880 Paris Conservatoire model offered the performer two, three and even four choices of ways to get the same note.

The oboe is a temperamental instrument—so much so that people used to believe that it drove its players crazy. The performer has a hard time breathing while keeping the air column flowing because he has to hold in his breath, rather than put all of it into the instrument. Often, you'll see that an oboist who has just finished playing first exhales before taking in a breath. The performer's control of his embouchure (use of mouth and tongue) is as important as his fingering in keeping the sound right. When an orchestra tunes, the oboe sounds the A for the other instruments to tune to. This is not because oboes make the finest A's: the oboe's pitch is affected by temperature, humidity, and the state of the reed, and the oboist can't easily tune it.

The Oboe

So, the other instruments adjust to the oboe.

Prokofiev uses the bassoon to represent Peter's grumbling grandfather. The bassoon, like other deep wind instruments, curves about. Somewhere in the late sixteenth century, someone realized that if you wound the tubes of wind instruments in curves or coils, you could keep the fingerholes within reach of the man who was blowing into the gadget, thus avoiding the need for two performers per instrument. The bassoon, for example, is a pipe 109 inches long (over nine feet). (If you want a deeper noise, you can get a contra-bassoon, which is sixteen feet long.) The bassoon hangs from a cord around the player's neck, and comes apart into five pieces: the crook (the little tube containing the double reed, into which the player blows); the wing joint (which goes down to the floor); the butt (the wooden u-bend at the bottom, like the bend in the pipe under your kitchen sink); the long joint (which comes up from the butt to above the player's head); and the bell, where the sound emerges after the player has finished manipulating the column of air. There's also a floor peg, coming from the butt, to rest some of the weight on the floor. A bassoonist needs unusual breath control, and his instrument can go out of tune easily, being very sensitive to changes in temperature. The bassoonist carries six to ten reeds, and often changes reeds during a performance when one deteriorates.

Around 1700 the bassoon had only four keys; by Beethoven's time it had eight, as its range extended upwards; and by the 1850's it had seventeen. Bassoons now often have twenty-two keys.

Peter's cat is represented by a clarinet, played staccato (with the notes sharply separated) in its lower register. The single reed of a clarinet vibrates against the slot in the mouthpiece. A performer can spend four to ten hours a week getting his reeds right.

The instrument wasn't widely used until after 1750, and was hard to play, but composers loved its sound. Mozart wrote his father, after hearing clarinets in the famous Mannheim orchestra, "If only we had clarinets. You can't guess the lordly effect of a symphony with flutes, oboes, and clarinets!" He used them often thereafter, and wrote a wonderful clarinet concerto.

The present clarinet, with thirteen keys, was standardized in the 1820's and 1830's; in 1843 Hyacinth Klose of the Paris Conservatoire reorganized the fingering in Boehm's manner.

Peter's wolf is represented by three horns playing chords in unison. The French horn is basically a sixteen-foot tube made of brass. (A tuba is thirty-five feet long—that's the big one!) It doesn't play an even scale. Horn players and horn makers spent many years trying to find ways to make one instrument play any note they wanted. Good embouchure helped, and some players learned to do wonders with mutes and hand-stopping the bell. Players used to carry extra crooks to insert in the tubing to lengthen the air column: but since 1818 a valve mechanism has been used, which allows the player to use

The Clarinet

The Bassoon

a lever or a button to work a rotary or piston valve, opening and shutting extra lengths of piping. With three valves, the hornist achieves his scale.

The horn is another tricky instrument, notoriously sensitive to temperature changes. Horn players sometimes do strange things with tape, matchsticks, and other makeshifts to make their instrument do what it ought. When it doesn't, everyone in the audience can usually hear the disaster. A misbehaving French horn can sound like a dying dinosaur.

Prokofiev also uses a trombone in *Peter and the Wolf*, although it is not assigned to any character. The slide trombone has been about the same since 1500. The player lengthens the column of air by moving the slide. Since the instrument is continuously adjustable, a player needs an exact ear to hit the notes, and not stop in between.

The only characters left to introduce are the three hunters, represented by the bass drum and kettle drums. They're part of the percussion section of the orchestra—instruments played by being hit. (You can count the piano as a percussion instrument, if you want to think of it that way.)

Percussion instruments have a long history. The tambourine, for example, seems to have been used by the Romans. Many different cultures have used drums in warfare. The kettle drums, which do look like large pots, have a pitch, which can be changed by hand (tightening or loosening the screws which put tension on the drum-head), or by a foot pedal, invented around 1830. The performer changes the quality of the tone by using different sticks and by muffling the drumheads.

The bass drum, which is two to three feet in diameter, has a thicker head, stretched less firmly than those of the kettledrums. Any percussionist needs a great sense of rhythm and split-second timing: when you hit an instrument that makes such noticeable noise, you'd better hit at exactly the right moment!

When you listen to *Peter and the Wolf*, you will realize that Prokofiev does not use an instrument only for the character it represents and that he uses instruments other than the character's principal instrument in writing music for that character.

At the beginning, for example, Peter's theme begins with the violins and violas, then extends downward into the deeper string sounds—cellos and double basses. The bird is introduced—first by the flute playing alone, but then the first violins, then the oboe, and finally the clarinet join in. Now the bird's theme combines itself with Peter's.

When the duck appears, the oboe is backed by the clarinet and bassoon as well as the violas; later the violins join, then the lower strings.

The violins warn us of the cat's intentions before we even begin to hear the clarinet sneaking along. The strings are plucked ("pizzicato") rather than bowed, to separate the notes sharply. Prokofiev deepens the sound by using the double basses under the deep clarinet sound. And, as the cat is about to pounce, and Peter shouts, "LOOK OUT!" we get the trumpet, a horn, and

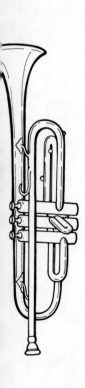

The Trumpet

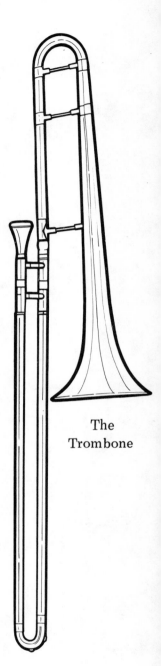

The
Trombone

cymbals all emphasizing the moment.

The bird's agitated twittering goes from the flute to the oboe, and the duck's quacking in the oboe is backed by the clarinet and bassoon. As the cat prowls around the tree, we hear the cymbals again, very lightly sounded.

When Grandfather comes out to lead Peter away, the bassoon has beneath it the bass drum, and we hear for the first time the theme of the wolf, as Grandfather warns Peter of the dangers he risks. The snare drum adds its sound, and the cymbals shimmer in the background.

When the wolf really appears, we get the three horns playing in unison at intervals, with cymbals, and occasionally the trombone and snare drums.

The snare drum helps chase the cat up the tree. As the wolf chases the cat and the duck, we don't hear the horns at all, till a brief suggestion comes when the wolf is catching up with the duck; then they sound out triumphantly as the duck is swallowed. The trumpet occasionally adds its notes to suggest the running wolf, and the trombone joins the horns and trumpet when the duck meets its fate.

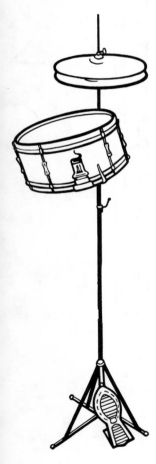

A Kettledrum

Then the cellos begin a little lament for the poor duck, and are joined by the oboe and other strings, then the low clarinet.

While the wolf prowls about beneath the tree, the clarinet has with it the cellos and double basses; a twitter from the flute reminds us of the bird; and the bass drum emphasizes the menace of the wolf. Again the horns are reinforced by cymbals and bass drum, as well as the low strings—cellos and double basses.

When Peter comes back into the action, his theme is reinforced by the bassoon—as if to suggest his grandfather is behind him.

While the bird flies around the wolf's head, we hear the triangle, then the snare drum. The horns and the trombone snap at the bird, helped by the trumpet, with snare drums and cymbals adding to the excitement.

All the winds, all the horns, all the strings, and the snare drum are now involved. Peter's lasso reduces the orchestra to first violins; then, as he catches the wolf, the sound goes to the cellos and double basses. The full sound returns as the wolf is caught—flute, oboe, clarinet, trumpet, horns, trombone, kettle drums, and snare drum, and all the strings but the basses.

The hunters enter the story to the sound of pizzicato strings, and the bass drum. As they shoot, we hear cymbals, and the winds, then the kettle drums. The snaredrum and the tambourine are also used, until Peter quiets the hunters.

During the triumphal procession, Peter's victory means that even the wolf's instruments join in playing Peter's theme. The one percussion instrument not yet used—the castanets—join in as part of the procession music.

Snare Drum & Cymbals